Leadership 20: A Team Building Card Game, By Tyler Hayden

Published by Tyler Hayden,
P.O. Box 1112
Lunenburg, Nova Scotia
Canada
B0J 2C0

Cover: Tyler Hayden
Illustrations & Page Design: Steven Lacey
Distributed Electronically by Kindle Direct Publishing

National Library of Canada Cataloguing in Publication

Hayden, Tyler, 1974–
        Leadership 20: A Team Building Card Game / Tyler Hayden.

ISBN   978-1-897050-55-2

Business. 2. Education. 3. Games. I. Title.

Discover More Fun @ www.teambuildingactivities.com

Leadership 20: A Team Building Card Game,
By Tyler Hayden

Warning - Use at Your Own Risk

Improper use of the contents described herein may result in serious injury or loss. The activities should not be attempted without the supervision of a trained and properly qualified leader.

FIND THIS FOR **FREE** ... WANT TO GIVE US A HIGH FIVE TO SAY THANK YOU?
We'd love you to BUY US A COFFEE or four - we like coffee.
www.teambuildingactivities.com/store/p46/donate

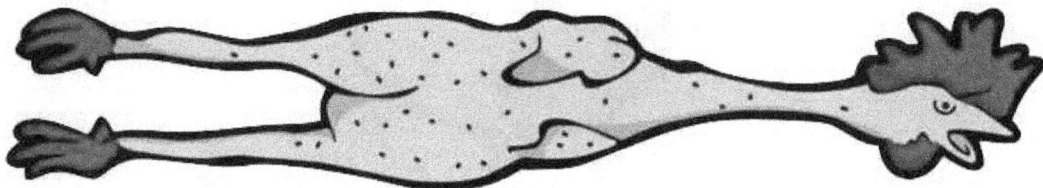

20 Series Games, By Tyler Hayden

This game takes about 10 to 25 minutes to play. It is an incredible content specific icebreaker/break-time activity that is totally inclusive. The educational intention is to encourage people to know a little more about each other in a fun and interactive way while learning a specific core content area (i.e. Customer Service, Leadership, etc). Check out our full line of Team 20 card decks at www.teambuildingactivities.com.

Remember, the priorities are to have fun and play safe.

How to play:

1. Make sure that you have a safe space for the participants to share. Schedule this activity at a time when they will be willing and open to talk to one another. I often run this event during a coffee break or to get the "cob webs" out part way through a meeting and focus the learners thoughts about our specific area of learning upcoming in our program. It is also great to pull it out when you are convening with a group you know fairly well, just for fun.

2. Place the game cards in the middle of the table along with a dice (if you don't have a dice download & make one at www.teammover.com/free).

3. The player with the longest commute goes first and rolls the dice. The person to the rollers right will pick up the card and ask the roller the question. If the player rolls a (1) a Who question is asked - (2) What; (3) When; (4) Where; (5) If; and (6) Why.

4. Once the question is read the roller answers the question. The answering is always "challenge by choice" meaning if they are uncomfortable with the question they answer. If not a new question can be drawn or they can pass on their turn.

5. Players around the table are permitted to ask follow-up questions to the person posing the answer as long as they relate to the original question asked.

6. Play continues sequentially in a clock wise direction.

7. There are two ways to "organize the play" – *Speed Version:* collectively the group answers the twenty questions total - keep track with a tally. *Longer Version:* each person answers a question from each category - keep track with a grid. Either way you need someone at the table keeping track of the "score".

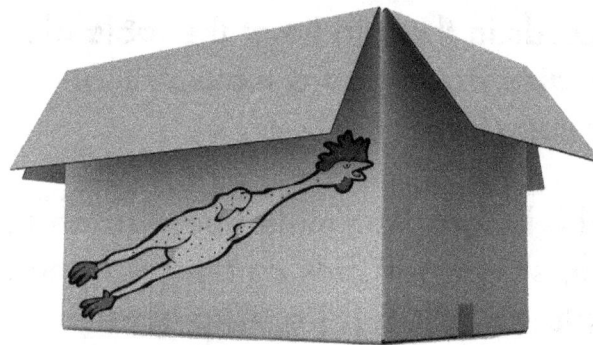

8. Have fun.

WHO 1	is your role model for leadership and why?
WHAT 2	matters more to good leadership, skill or luck?
WHEN 3	people meet you what do you want them to say about you?
WHERE 4	have you received the best leadership training?
HOW 5	you could recommend any book to develop leadership skills, what would it be?
WHY 6	is being a "leader" a thankless job?

© Tyler Hayden

WHO 1	has the toughest leadership role in the world?
WHAT 2	is the most admirable quality of a leader?
WHEN 3	was the biggest leadership mistake in the history of the world?
WHERE 4	should a leader start when delivering bad news about a project?
HOW 5	you had to suggest an animal that possessed your leadership traits, what animal is it?
WHY 6	is leadership a gift that is given by the team?

© Tyler Hayden

WHO 1	has had to make the hardest leadership decision of all time?
WHAT 2	did your best boss teach you about leadership?
WHEN 3	is a time when a leader should leave their post or team?
WHERE 4	have you found a high concentration of good leaders within a single business?
HOW 5	you were to build a leader's walk of fame, who would belong on it?
WHY 6	do good leaders burn out?

© Tyler Hayden

WHO 1	should never have been allowed to be a leader of a country?
WHAT 2	life event taught you the most powerful leadership lesson?
WHEN 3	did a leader say something profound to you? What was it?
WHERE 4	do you find good experiences to develop your leadership skills?
HOW 5	you were to teach your children one leadership skill, what would it be?
WHY 6	do leaders fail?

© Tyler Hayden

WHO **1**	do you know who leads authentically?
WHAT **2**	is your greatest leadership skill?
WHEN **3**	did you wish a certain had more time to lead in their position?
WHERE **4**	should a new staff member look to enhance their skills?
HOW **5**	you had to elect one person leader of your country, who would you choose?
WHY **6**	are leaders great?

© Tyler Hayden

WHO **1**	epitomizes fair leadership?
WHAT **2**	is the hardest leadership lesson you have had to make?
WHEN **3**	have you experienced poor leadership?
WHERE **4**	should you assign dysfunctional team members?
HOW **5**	a family pet was ever leading a project you were on, which pet deserves the honor?
WHY **6**	is political leadership such a balancing act?

© Tyler Hayden

WHO 1	is an unsung leader that you know?
WHAT 2	is the greatest gift a leader can give?
WHEN 3	is it evident that a leader is not best fit for a certain group?
WHERE 4	is the best place to get advice/guidance as a team leader?
HOW 5	money were no object, what experience would improve your skills?
WHY 6	do you like being a leader?

© Tyler Hayden

WHO 1	possesses a leadership skill that you admire? And what is that skill?
WHAT 2	TV show or movie teaches the best leadership lesson?
WHEN 3	do you lead from behind?
WHERE 4	do you go to go relax when the stressors of leadership get to you?
HOW 5	you could work for one media personality, who would it be?
WHY 6	do leaders need content knowledge for work teams?

© Tyler Hayden

WHO 1	**is the best sports team leader of all time?**
WHAT 2	**was the single greatest leader of all time?**
WHEN 3	**is it OK to admit you were wrong as a leader?**
WHERE 4	**did you work on the best team of all time?**
HOW 5	**one Disney character was your boss, which one would you want it to be?**
WHY 6	**are leaders needed in a virtual team?**

© Tyler Hayden

WHO **1**	leads without a title?
WHAT **2**	three leadership skills should ever child be taught?
WHEN **3**	is it not OK to admit you were wrong as a leader?
WHERE **4**	is direct leadership not required at your work?
HOW **5**	you were given one reward for a job well done, what would it be?
WHY **6**	are leaders different in today's business world?

© Tyler Hayden

WHO 1	**is a leader who empowers their group to achieve more?**
WHAT 2	**matters more a leaders title or how they conduct themselves?**
WHEN 3	**should you consider succession planning of a leadership role?**
WHERE 4	**should leaders place their energy - low or high team performers?**
HOW 5	**your mom ran the company, what would she insist on changing?**
WHY 6	**do you respect a leader?** © Tyler Hayden

WHO 1	opened your eyes to great leadership?
WHAT 2	leader would you "follow" anywhere?
WHEN 3	should you promote someone into a leadership position?
WHERE 4	should you look to find a leadership mentoring opportunity?
HOW 5	you could choose, would you skydive or drive NASCAR?
WHY 6	do you "write off" a leader?

© Tyler Hayden

WHO 1	**is a leader you would like to have as a mentor?**
WHAT 2	**leadership skills did your parents teach you?**
WHEN 3	**should a leader be fired?**
WHERE 4	**is the coolest place a leader has ever hosted a meeting you attended?**
HOW 5	**you had to describe the perfect leadership traits, what would they be?**
WHY 6	**are leaders "motivational"?**

© Tyler Hayden

WHO **1**	has a special skill in leadership that you have seen in action at this table?
WHAT **2**	leadership skills did you learn playing as a kid?
WHEN **3**	is your favorite time to lead a group within a project cycle?
WHERE **4**	is the best place to get rewards for your staff?
HOW **5**	you could trade places with one leader for a day, who would it be?
WHY **6**	do leaders need to learn leadership skills?

© Tyler Hayden

WHO 1	makes you want to achieve more?
WHAT 2	organization would you like to lead?
WHEN 3	should a leader reward an individual within a team? and How?
WHERE 4	is the best place to get you a gift card from as a reward?
HOW 5	you could change one law, what would it be?
WHY 6	is it important for leaders to have a mentor?

© Tyler Hayden

WHO 1	inspires you?
WHAT 2	leadership skill should every CEO have?
WHEN 3	when should a leader recognize individuals who exceeded expectations?
WHERE 4	would be the most horrifying place to "do a team building event" for you?
HOW 5	leaders all demonstrated "this" trait the world would be a better place.
WHY 6	is leadership a lonely job?

© Tyler Hayden

WHO 1	makes you mad every time you hear them speak?
WHAT 2	leadership trait is most important to be successful in your job?
WHEN 3	is it OK for a leader to confront a dysfunctional team member?
WHERE 4	would you like to go for a team building event with this group?
HOW 5	you could have dinner with one media personality, who would it be?
WHY 6	is leadership stressful?

© Tyler Hayden

WHO 1	is a natural leader in your family?
WHAT 2	behaviors create a trustworthy leader?
WHEN 3	have you made a stand as a leader for the good of your team?
WHERE 4	would be the best place to host a team celebration?
HOW 5	you were to be stuck in a mine shaft with one historical leader, who would it be?
WHY 6	is leadership the best job in the world?

© Tyler Hayden

WHO 1	works harder the leader or the team?
WHAT 2	traits in a leader really turn you off?
WHEN 3	have you lost it as a leader?
WHERE 4	are our gaps right now at work?
HOW 5	you could transport through time, who would you like to have coffee with?
WHY 6	is leadership often shared in teams?

© Tyler Hayden

WHO **1**	should set the tone for work flow?
WHAT **2**	does a leader have to do to inspire you?
WHEN **3**	did you feel you had the best functioning team of all time?
WHERE **4**	are our advantages right now at work?
HOW **5**	our government made "this" change, we would be in a better place.
WHY **6**	should a leaders collaborate with their team?

© Tyler Hayden

WHO **1**	inspired your career path?
WHAT **2**	is better a leader who pushes you or pulls you towards goals?
WHEN **3**	did you wish you had a do over as a leader?
WHERE **4**	did you learn good traits of leadership?
HOW **5**	you could work for one great leader who would it be?
WHY **6**	is being _____ the most important leadership quality?

© Tyler Hayden

WHO **1**	has it harder, a leader of a dysfunctional team or a high performance team?
WHAT **2**	is your favorite leadership quote?
WHEN **3**	does a leader know enough to guide a group?
WHERE **4**	generally are emerging leaders gaps in knowledge or skill?
HOW **5**	a leader wants more out of their team, they should...
WHY **6**	should leaders invest time in knowing their team?

© Tyler Hayden

WHO 1	in history is a leader you would have liked to have dinner with?
WHAT 2	traits are foundational for a leader?
WHEN 3	should a leader direct actions of a team?
WHERE 4	could senior leaders learn a thing or two from emerging leaders?
HOW 5	a person wants to be noticed by their boss they should...
WHY 6	do bad leaders get promoted to leadership roles?

© Tyler Hayden

WHO 1	has the qualities of a leader a dog or a cat?
WHAT 2	skills are essential for any good leader?
WHEN 3	should you facilitate actions of your team?
WHERE 4	have you been on the best team?
HOW 5	I were to develop one leadership skill it would be...
WHY 6	are you ready to take on a project leadership role?

© Tyler Hayden

WHO 1	taught you an important leadership lesson? What was it?
WHAT 2	leadership skills would you like to develop?
WHEN 3	is collaboration a good practice? and a bad practice?
WHERE 4	is your happy place?
HOW 5	I could be mentored by one leader alive or dead, it would be ...
WHY 6	is _____ the best leader of all time?

© Tyler Hayden

A Message for you.

Dear Team Mover,

We are so thankful you chose to share one of our 20 Series Books with your Team. We are passionate about helping connect people in meaningful ways by brining the world books, activities and tools like this - because we think people matter.

As we move forward in publishing this (and other) series of books and games, we need your help to build a community of people with that same authentic desire to create meaningful relationships with the people they work with. We ask you join us and share our work with your friends, colleagues and families.

Here are some of the ways that we can stay connected and you can find more resources (link to the appropriate social media links on the sites):

Team Building - www.teambuildingactivities.com
Keynotes & Consulting - www.tylerhayden.com
Books & Consulting - www.14minutementor.com
Books & Giving - www.messageinabottlebook.com

Look forward to connecting soon. Best of continued success my fellow team mover - the work you are doing matters.

Tyler